CONTINUING CONCLUSIONS

Other Poetry by Richmond Lattimore

Poems (1957)
Sestina for a Far-off Summer (1962)
The Stride of Time (1966)
Poems from Three Decades (1972)

CONTINUING CONCLUSIONS

New Poems and Translations by

RICHMOND LATTIMORE

Louisiana State University Press
Baton Rouge and London
1983

For Frederick Morgan

Design: Albert Crochet
Typeface: Linotron Galliard
Typesetter: G & S Typesetters, Inc.
Printer: Thomson-Shore, Inc.
Binder: John H. Dekker & Sons, Inc.

LIBRARY OF CONGRESS CATALOGING IN PUBLICATION DATA
Lattimore, Richmond Alexander, 1906–
    Continuing conclusions.

    I. Title.
PS3523.A775C6   1983   811'.52   83-727
ISBN 0-8071-1083-3
ISBN 0-8071-1084-1 (pbk.)

Grateful acknowledgment is made to the publications in which
some of these poems first appeared:
"In the Café" and "Candles" in *American Poetry Review*;
"Disadvantages" in *For Rexroth . . . The Ark* 14; "Rondeau" and
"To Charles, Duke of Orleans" in *Boston University Journal*; "Les
Folies Françaises, ou les Dominos," "Spanish Succession," "Daisy
Fields, Enchanted Forests," "Of Truth and Fact," "Protoprimavera,"
"Noon," "Sonnet Addressed to Henry III," "Night Travel,"
"Riviera Railway," "The Islands," "Former Residence,"
"Shanhaikuan," "They Used To Have a Homecoming Day,"
"Aspects of Time," and "Home" in *Hudson Review*; "The Rage of
Demeter" in *Richard Eberhart: A Celebration*; "Gehenna" in *The
New Yorker* (June 6, p. 129), copyright © 1977, The New Yorker
Magazine, Inc.; "Painter" in *Pearl*; "Blood Relations" in
Philadelphia Poets; "Flesh Tones," "Bone Structure," "Coastal
Stuff," "Western Ways," "Sliding Scales," and "The Pearl" in
Poetry; "Form and Actuality," "Winter Return," and "The Elite" in
Poetry Northwest; "Monadology" in *Press*; "Fall Guise" in *The
Sound of a Few Leaves*; "The Elephants" in *Southern Review*; "Tales
from the Father of History" (January 1, 1982), in *Times Literary
Supplement*; "Forlorn Dream Song" in *A Tumult for John
Berryman*; "Waves" in *The Water of Light*, copyright © 1976,
University of Utah Press.

Contents

III

I

Former Residence

Roof shot with holes,
boards blinding
windows, lawn a waste
of broken concrete and
rubble, only the steel
ball and the terminal
crunch left to wait
and fear. That's all.

                    Here
we lived, ate
loved drank
had babies had friends had a
ball.
       It's a crate, full
of smashed floors,
lost nails, bruised slats,
dry pipes, dust, rats, the
place is full of frail
hopes, fond looks, blown
cools, fashions friends
festivities, sweets and
successors and now
silences. All ends.

Tales of Hoffmann

Broken doll elusive broad breathless singer,
you live on gin tobacco and impatience
my wife my muse my
life: oh, your angelic raves that make no sense:

most losing: more in fevers, less
in hard health. Oh, why
has it got to be such an exhausting business?
Despair of captures and you're suddenly

there. Anything but let me alone.
What am I left to keep?
Hoffmann his triform Stella and slugged sleep.
Joseph his Mary moments. I my own.

Isabel

When you wore shell-rims, they looked too old for you.
When you bobbed your hair, they said it was too much.
No girl should look so delightful.
You broke the hearts of the 15th Infantry
and the California students and stayed free
as an angel. Fifty years and three husbands later
you were still my wise little older sister,
patient in pain and amusing
until the last indignities as a speechless shape on the bed.
So even the Lattimore children have to die.
There was a time we thought we were all immortal.

Riviera Railway

The nice conductor prayed people to be gentile
and let us into the compartment. They didn't. There were in fact
three persons, and two soldiers had their coats laid

on the window seats as they themselves stood in the corridor
and admired the view and blocked passage. It rained daylong.
We both had colds. Change at Florence and change

again at Pisa. Arno swollen and angry,
no tower in sight, only the crowds. No food, no
diner, but we had buns saved over and a fiasco

of Chianti white. This made cocktails, dinner,
port and brandy as we stood in the back vestibule, next to
the double latrine and the kidney smell. Strung out

a long drizzled day, color of rain, standing
and waiting. Night now. Breaks in the rock-slot flashed us
snug harbors, rainy sea-view benches under the heel

of the train, lights green and red wet slipping
on the black. This is our life. Due at 8, on the stroke
of midnight reached Genoa and got off at the wrong station.

Painter

The visible world is at your disposal. Seas and cities,
landscapes wooded or open, skyscapes, people draped
or bare. You can make a creation out of a bowl

of African violets, a string chair, eggs, spoons, a billiard table,
and if all fails paint your own face. Godlike. But the making
of divine power was no breeze. To learn the secrets

of paints, their combinations. Hours a day
for months copying casts. The training of eye
mind and hand to make the convergence of lines more real than life is.

Rude or sharp, subtle or coarse, the difficultly fashioned master of the
visible world.

Shanhaikuan

Out there, the horizon smudged with smoke of the little freighters.
Inshore, the transparent shallows and the ribbed brown floor.
South, the flat beach draws its line firm to the edge of distance.

The beach ends north in a point of rocks where baby waves slip
and wash back and gurgle; and jumbled in the rocks slabs of big and
    broken
stones. These are the last stones of the Great Wall, which loped

over the unsung hills and mountains of North China, and staggered
and broke up into the blue Gulf. Beyond, it is Manchuria.
Another country. But on the near shore, children playing.

They rode down to swims and games on a little horse-drawn trolley
which links the beach with the station and the small foreign settlement.
There is the long two-story hotel with its wide veranda,

the spaces of its dining and bedrooms, the deferential
long-gowned servants, the menus, with lists of champagnes and clarets,
its tennis courts, and the baron with the underhand serve.

Inland from the tracks is a Chinese city, small but
as walled as Peking, with gates towers and battlements;
and far above are the bulging cliffs, the saddle where the Great Wall

of China drapes away toward Jehol. And from one height
the dizzy downlook gave a secret valley, nestling
one tiny and complete and inaccessible temple.

Winter Return

Gray bridge to the Albany towers shaped
on a turbid sky, and here in the snow cold men
lug over and fling down heavy spikes of black iron.

I watch from behind a frosted window, night-shaken.
What ever became of the water-level route?
The sleeper bounced like an old Peking cart

in a hurry, banging me loose from memory. One more
nail knocked out of its hole. For my fatigue and indifference
rails, men, and spikes, black and white display in the snow.

The Elite

"Lattimore gives us the whole bag" (Some reviewer or other)

If you knew the half of it: my fifty years of trash cans
waste baskets burn bags; the finished duds; stillborns; the embarrassing
juvenilia; the more shaming senescences; the too-personal;

the hurtful poems; the self-generated productions
of thought hateful or rejected; the merely dated or obsolete
self, gone poesies, bad Swinburne. Lost hours, spent labor.

A poet has to be his own ragpicker. I will not be immodest.
But if you knew what prides and pleasures got pitched. My makings.
Now, somewhat survives and is saved as worlds turn to garbage.

Saved. Cream or scum. But there was skimming.

They Used to Have a Homecoming Day

End of a hot day's drive on unimaginative
straight roads over the flat of the huge midland with its too much
corn; and the names come out of my past, Mahomet, the Sangamon,

Champaign-Urbana; threading the difficult point-to-point of U.S.
46. What a way to come back or not quite to
come back. Race and Green gloomed up, then the colossal

stadium. So to our motel. Phone book. No names, they must all
be dead. Unseen, Lincoln Hall, where I studied, where I taught Latin
and Philosophy, and sweated it out, and knew my future.

Shapes in the mist, shot by and lost. Flat streets, the rented
rooms, skinny breakfasts. Kicking leaves on the sidewalks.
The Press, alien now and I'm grumpy. Good-bye Urbana.

Known territory glimpsed gone. No instant, no deferred replay.

Daisy Fields, Enchanted Forests

What's in our past
That we can call our own?
Some of our leaves are lost,
some fields are overgrown.

The meadows dipped and rolled
away to the hillside,
our daisy fields of old,
and one elm in her pride.

There was a track below
the quarry with its rail.
There is no quarry now.
There is no trail.

Strangest of all
has grown a suburb, split-
levels where hills were tall
with trees. It

invades the daisy meadow,
and where the elm stood
tall with its proud shadow,
has grown the peopled wood

where we'll no more. All lost,
the meadow where we strolled,
the fields we crossed.
And can I be so old?

Coastal Stuff

Rain slopping down for hours curdled
the steam from a little dockside switcher to fat white
clouds, greasy blossoms bunching. Beyond, gray water,

until just in time to set the sun turned
on like a lamp. We ventured the pleasantly
pigsy centre of Civitavecchia, stepping

around puddles. In a cordial tavern a fat girl
who fondled a doll served us martinis in almost
buckets, before we dined in the vast shining

sala di pranzo of the Mediterranée Suisse,
uninhabited except for waiters sleek in
black and white. Then out to the heights

to watch the steamer in from Olbia.
Torn-up clouds and gray waste of water.
Little cars like wet bugs on the sluiced dockside.

Then rain came down again and clammed us back into our castle.

Night Travel

Heave our bags up the high
steps, wrestle corridor and rack, col-
lapse briefly on cushions, and the train
slides into black, glides into its pitch
and roll, tries to soar (bird on rails), wheels
on in gathering speed, throwing
Italian names back into the dark, throwing switch
and points, lights, posto di blocco, discarded
stations, throwing a shatter of thoughts, throwing
our past, or our presence, away.
                          Here
we are again where we were, where
this has been going on year after year
when we weren't here (but how could it?) but now here
we are, with nonpotable aqua, action the chase-
water and bat back the covercle, here in place
of our lives ago in a slot
of rails and time. What
are we here for? Searching, forgetting, escaping
here in the lurching
night as our progress from now into next throws
the names away behind us into what bin
of oblivion? Who knows? But here
where we've been, we are.

Sliding Scales

Skin bones and gristle, blood and fats, all essential organs
and features recycled and reconstituted over and over
again. Not nearly as good as new. Dislike of mirrors.

But never mind all my accidents of carnal corruption.
Something is same while everything about it is other.
What makes it same? It isn't the pile of stuffs, a pile of

other stuffs every moment, that made it through sixty years plus
ten to now. What now? Now's gone already. But I'm here
still if not for long. Still skin bones gristle and the rest of

the catalogue. Plus substance. That is the never-made-of-
material question still, and still in my head an imperfect
philosopher walks with Descartes and Kant and ponders the timeless.

A Marriage

We are made of scenes nights screens pursuits
and flights, corridors and chasms, and I remember
once how you fled into future and, following,

how I caught the train up that coast, sleepless
head on aching arm to a desolate station,
and floated like a shell through those daylong streets,

lost lost and my true love gone into never. Life in a capsule
of fugitive wheels and black and gold of the night coast.
Love lost across water and I alone on the shore.

Did it every happen? Neither could you endure it,
but entreated me back. Now forty-five years gone,
how many friends rides trains deaths since;

babies grown, rifts lived down and forgotten, houses
outlived: all but the love: we live for
our narrowing future, pass the parlor and wonder

which of us two will have to bury the other.

II

The Elephants

From the French of Leconte de Lisle

The red sand like an ocean spreads in wastes afar,
blazing and stunned upon its bed, immense and mute,
to where the skyline, quivering and absolute,
reflects that coppery haze that comes where people are.

No life is there, no sound. Now all the lions, full
of food, a hundred leagues away sleep in their caves,
as the giraffe drinks from the blue and springing waves
under far date palms which the panthers know so well.

No single bird disturbs the sky with wings, or sails
that dense air where the sun makes his enormous round.
Sometimes perhaps some boa, chafed by the hot ground,
writhes in his sleep and shudders his fantastic scales.

Under clear skies, this is the burning world of sand.
But while all else sleeps through the dismal solitude,
the elephants, slow travelers, wrinkled and rude,
cross the great desert to regain their native land.

From the horizon moving as a mass of brown
they come, raising a cloud of dust, and one might see
how, on a line of march as straight as it can be,
their large and certain feet trample the sand dunes down.

An old chief marches at their head. His body, frayed
and scored, is like a tree that wind and weather wrack.
His head is like a boulder, and his arching back
powerfully contracts with every motion made.

Never delaying, never hastening his march,
he guides toward their sure journey's end his dusty band,
and, leaving in their wake a trampled trough of sand,
the massive pilgrims follow their great patriarch.

Trunk fast between the tusks, eyes closed, and great ears spread
like fans, they trudge along. The belly steams and sighs,
and from the vapor of their sweat a cloud of flies
rises to swarm and hover about every head.

But what to them are flies and thirst and weariness,
or that their brown and wrinkled backs burn in the sun?
They dream along their journey of a land once known,
the forest fig trees, ancient cradle of their race.

And they shall see the mountain-risen stream once more,
where the huge hippo swims and bellows as he plays,
where underneath the moon and outlined in her rays
they came to drink, wrecking the reeds along the shore.

And so they pass, deliberate and free from fear,
like a black line across the everlasting sand,
which now resumes its stillness as the ponderous band
of travelers merges in skyline, and disappears.

Gaiezza Annuale

From the English of Wallace Stevens

Nella mattina nella neve azzurra
Il sole cattolico, la sua maestà
Arrosisce e arrosisce la melanconia ghiacciodura.

Ma perché queste preghiere alla luna?
O è perché gli alligatori giacciono
Lunge i margini del tuo occhio
Scaldandosi nella Florida deserta?

Papa Guzz, in cielo, tocca la tua lira,
E canta il fuoco gennaiale
E la gioia di neve e neve.

Sonnet Addressed to Henry III
on the Death of Thulène, the King's Fool

From the French of Jean Passerat

Thulène is dead, my lord. I saw his funeral.
But it is in your power to bring him back again.
Appoint some poet to inherit his domain.
Poets and fools are of the same material.
One scorns advancement. One has nowhere to advance.
In both accounts, the gain is greater than the loss.
Both kinds are quick to anger, difficult to cross.
One speaks on impulse, one leaves everything to chance.
One is light-headed, but the other one is seen
wearing a pretty cap and bells, yellow and green.
One sings his rhymes, the other capers to his chimes.
Yet we are different in one important way.
Fortune has always favored fools, or so they say.
She's seldom favored poets in the best of times.

Noon

From the French of Leconte de Lisle

Noon, summer king, descending from the skyblue height,
in silver shimmers spreads across the entire plain,
and all is quiet. The air burns, breathless and bright,
and the land clothed in fire dreams under his domain.

The scope is huge. There is no shadow anywhere.
The spring is dried where once the cattle could drink deep,
and, dark about the edge, the forest over there
rests in its immobility of heavy sleep.

Only the great ripe heads of grain, a golden sea,
untouched by sleep, roll into distance and away.
Pacific children of blest earth's fertility,
these freely drink the sunshine from the bowl of day.

And sometimes from this murmuring and heavy grain,
as if the ardent soul within had sighed aloud,
a slow majestic ripple goes across the plain
to die on the horizon's dusty haze of cloud.

Nearby, lazily dribbling on dewlaps, a few
cream-colored oxen lie at rest along the grass,
and with their great eyes, languid and superb, pursue
the inward dream that they will never bring to pass.

Oh, you who with heart full of joy or bitterness
may chance to pass at noon across this radiant plain,
depart! Here the sun burns; nature is emptiness.
Here nothing lives. Nothing feels pleasure here, nor pain.

But if, beyond all laughter and all tears, you live
free from that troubled world whence you have taken flight,
with nothing to condemn and nothing to forgive,
and wish to taste one final and austere delight,

come! Listen to the sun's sublime discourse; and when
you have given yourself to its relentless majesty,
slowly retrace your steps to the mean cities of men,
heart seven times steeped in the divine nonentity.

In the Café

From the Greek of Constantine Cavafy

Inside the noisy café at noon
sits an old man at a table apart from the rest.
A newspaper is in front of him. No one is with him.

And in the contempt of wretched old age, he considers
how little joy there was for him in those years
when he had strength, and wit, and looks.

He knows that he has aged greatly. He feels it, he sees it.
And with all that, the time when he was young seems
as if it were yesterday. How small, how small the interval.

He thinks of Prudence, how she mocked him.
and how he entrusted everything (how silly!)
to the traitress who said: "Tomorrow. You have plenty of time."

He thinks of longings he repressed, all the pleasures
he sacrificed. Like lost happiness
everything mocks, now, his diminished senses.

But with thinking and remembering too much
the old man grows tired. He leans his elbows
over the café table, and goes to sleep.

Candles

From the Greek of Constantine Cavafy

The days of the future are standing before me
like a row of lighted candles:
golden hot living candles.

The past days remain behind me,
a sad line of spent candles;
the nearest ones still give off smoke.
Cold candles, melted down, bent.

I don't want to look at them; the sight of them pains me,
and I am pained to think of the light they once had.
I look forward at my lighted candles.

I don't want to turn around and see, with a shudder,
how quickly the dark line lengthens,
how quickly the spent candles multiply.

Quand nous habitions tous . . .

From the French of Victor Hugo: Two Versions

A

When we lived all of us together
in our hills of yesterday,
by clear streams and tossing heather
in the house by the forest way,

I was thirty. She was ten.
I was her world, her all.
How fragrant the grass grows, when
above it the trees stand tall.

She gave me prosperity.
Skies were blue, work was like play.
When she said "Father" to me,
"My Goddess" was all I could say.

Through my incessant daydreams
I could hear her happy replies.
My face grew less dark for the gleams
that shone from her eyes.

She was a princess whenever
we walked on the road hand in hand.
She went looking for flowers forever,
and for someone poor to befriend,

for she gave, as if given, for pity,
but hid her kindnesses from all.
That little dress! How pretty
it was. Do you recall?

She would chatter in a soft voice
next my candle at night,
while the night moths tapped their noise
on the pane where it glowed with light.

Angels preened in her skies.
Her "good morning" was charming to hear.

Heaven had given her eyes
forever true and sincere.

So young, yet I had known
she was part of my destiny.
She was the child of my dawn,
and the morning star for me.

When the moon shone clear and bright
through that time's serenities,
how we would walk at night;
how we would run through the trees!

There was one lonely gleam
in the dark house. That was all.
We would come back by the stream
at the angle of the old wall.

Reliving, with hearts on fire,
the sky's glories, we would come home.
I formed her young character
as the honey-bee builds her comb.

Sweet angel, she was so gay
on returning: white thoughts, pure mind.
Those times are all blown away
like shadow, like wind.

B

There was a time when we lived all together
in our hills of long ago, by running streams
and shivering leaves in the house at the edge of the woods.

She was ten, I was thirty. I was all the world
for her. Oh, how fresh the smell of the grass
when the tall trees above it are deep and green.

She made my fortunes prosper, she made my labors
light, and my skies blue. When she called me "father,"
all my heart could answer with was "my goddess."

Through my innumerable daydreams I listened
to her happy chatter, and my face that was in the shadow
would be illuminated from her eyes' shining.

She had the air of a princess when we went walking
together hand in hand. She was always looking
for flowers by the way, and for poor people, so she could help them.

She gave the way others take, but tried to keep hidden
the good she did so none might see. Oh, the little
dress she wore, how pretty. Do you remember?

In the evening, by my candle light, she would murmur
softly to herself while the night-moths battered
themselves against the glowing pane of the window.

Angels preened in her. How enchanting her good-
morning greetings. Her eyes were endowed by heaven
with that kind of look that can give no falsehood.

So young, and yet I had already seen how she
was a part of my destiny. She was the daughter
of my dawn, and she was my morning star.

When the moon, serene and clear, shone in the skies of
all those happy days, how we would wander
about the meadows. How we would run in the forest.

Then, toward that solitary light that illumined
like a star the dark house, we would come returning
by the valley, and turn the old wall at the corner:

come back with our hearts full of fire, recalling
all the glories of the sky. I was forming
this young soul, the way the bee makes its honey.

Sweet angel with pure thoughts, her arrivals always
were full of happiness. Now all these things are past
and gone from us, like a shadow, and like the wind.

Castel Galante

From the English of Wallace Stevens

E malo esser qui arrivato
E aver trovato vido il letto?

Si poteva trovar capille tragiche,
Occhi amari, mane nimiche, gelide.

Si poteva esser una luce sopr' uno libro
Illuminanda una-due verse senza pietà.

Si poteva esser la solitudine immensa
Del venta contra le cortine.

Verse senza pietà? Qualche parole accordate
Accordate accordate accordate.

E buono. E vido il letto.
Le cortine sono rigide e formale e calme.

Psara

From the Greek of Dionysios Solomos

On the black spine of Psara
the lonely Glory, walking by herself,
thinks of her shining young men; and on her hair
she wears a garland made
out of that scanty grass that still
remained upon this barren ground.

Rondeau

From the French of Charles, Duke of Orleans

God, who made her, look upon her,
gracious good and beautiful.
For her gifts so bountiful,
all are fain to do her honor.
What man could abandon her,
every day more wonderful?
God, who made her, look upon her,
gracious good and beautiful.
On the near or farther shore
I can name no demoiselle
so completely worshipful.
It's a dream to think upon her.
God, who made her, look upon her.

To Charles, Duke of Orleans

One of their inept chivalry on the field
of Agincourt, amidst the shambles there,
you had the ordinary sense to yield,
the good luck to be taken prisoner,
and in exiled defeated circumstance
inactive, free from misdirected honor,
you gazed from Dover at the shores of France,
and wrote, o God, who made her, look upon her.
Among your butcherly peers, you, rapt in rhyme,
wizard of rondeaux, you, almost alone,
shine, if with a quieter flame than Joan,
as one clean light in a foul time.

III

Gehenna

Truly a cursed place, but hell fire? That would be brighter
and consume, kill and purify. These acres are rather
the dump, that cries aloud for landfill. Here fires slow-burn,

smoulder, do not flame, and in the forbidden pit and the outcast
offal see maggots breed and wriggle. This is our worm un-
dying. Here where once they burned the babies for Moloch

the fires are never quenched and never burn out, contaminate
and do not cleanse ever the rainless refuse of evil.
Is this what everyman must walk over so as to accomplish

the shining hills on the other side, the far green arches
and clear floors in the still not unattainable forest?
Got to do it on foot, and hurting.

The Rage of Demeter

(The cement works at Eleusis)
For Richard Eberhart

As on a stalled and stranded liner, four
great stacks stand at the corner of the plain, and pour
thick yellow smoke, night and day, day
and night, to plague and poison breath.
Those beautiful, those lapis lazuli blue,
those numb, those cankered waters now
are crammed and cluttered, prow on rotting prow
with derelict freighters, tankers,
cast-off landing-craft dying on their anchors.
Trade's sad garbage.

                    Once there came
as a wind blown light and bitter from the sky
the orphaned and resentful goddess. Day was night.
For a lost child she cursed the world to die.
The bud stiffened in calyx, and the blight
seared children, until high gods must convene,
reshape a world to save it and restore
a seasonal daughter now become the queen
of death.

              So life and death combine.

                         Grain
dies to live. The indiscriminate masses come
their dull ways to her mystery. There they found
the well of indifference, the well of memory,
each by the wayside groves of underground.
Souls spoke their rites of drama. Mum-
bled prayers, so they shall die and live again.

Between, between
the layers of rage, the hatreds, the old sores,
the trample of invasions, the sour wars,
are intervals of gold and green,
rock and tree, the green and golden grain,
the times of chapeled hills, the times of flowers

and bells, the moments held and seized as ours.
And then the cycle turns and all is lost again.

Why, once more, must it happen? The curse comes now.
Old symbols are enacted in the gain
of greed, the greed of gain. Imbalance scores
the world with fault. The necessary death
outweighs necessity. Demeter pours
from her four stacks that poisoned yellow breath
over the strait toward Athens. Oh, forgive
the world once more, Demeter. Let us live.

Lesefruchte

In this more mortal time
of life, I wonder, how did the acknowledged great,
the acclaimed, the achieved,
face their dimming futures, their meager late
few flowers to come, grieved
for lost senses.

                  Instance. Book Review Section. Photo.
See the Great Man arrived
at airport station or pier,
dignified aged dried austere,
somewhat dumpily wived
by the faithful *Frau* beside
him. And the sober head carries inside
its bonehouse, what?

                  Memory of what made
magic? Walpurgis Mountain: the sad
and sober with the mournful and the mad
and merry: the bony goggle-eyed tall
doctor: the sallow strong tender psychiatrist:
the people of the Mountain:
and beyond all
recall
from memory, the mountain, and the mist,
and summon to arise
the pale young German with the simple blue eyes,
those Russian girls, and one forever gazed
upon, the slattern with the lovely arms
and over-the-shoulder glance that mocked the dazed
blue eyes, her honey hair, the charms
of her slurred French.

                  Was it all so, or made
of the mind in a book? Now, mated
to one of those ugly dumplings the German swan
girls grow into, what's real for him, the stated

tale, or remembered life
in his ultimate Switzerland or Palisade?
Life is the book.

               Even I, man and wife
with my still-swan, remember what I could
not make into a classic if I would,
in this gray time, the touch and taste of life.

      Postscript

Got it all wrong. He was a mere fifty-five,
mid-career still and very much alive.
Unfair to the *Frau* too. It's the *hat*. Yet still,
how little like the belle of Daghestan,
how little like the pale young man
on the enchanted hill.

Home

Corridors, carpets, and closed glass, wheelchairs,
and the little steps and canes, and the nurse's arm for those who
went once as powerful men, firm women: all this

wreckage of past perfections: physical all washed out and the spirit
only left: quiet, sealed temperatures: the carefully
preserved. Bit by bit I have seen it coming, in mirrors.

No brink, a gentle progress some guy up there has decreed was for
us. A decade or so now left. As elderly visitor
I walk through this as a young man walks and know what I'm in for.

Fragments of the imagination of God and his handiwork.

Forlorn Dream Song

For John Berryman

This cat never knew
that one, won't never no how now.
But why people go stand on a bridge, teeter
& jump? Whoo,
no way to live. Oh never now
unless somewhere somehow

on a bridge of cloud Peter
slosh us out martinis now for two.
And Henry had it made.
How ever you dream up that metre?
Dropped like a Virgin into your lap? You
got it said.

Meditated on what & went & did it.
Oh we got poets yes we got em still.
There 6s all 4s.
Waiting in line we stand & fidget
for heaven or hell.
Nemmine us, Mr. Bones. No. You got yours.

Return to the Light

White heels flash shortly up the air,
the head descending hits the green
and greener turning water where
pebbles subluminous are seen

pale in the sand, and sunless stone,
and shreds in the coolness, and the swarms
of running bubbles backward blown,
and as the green and twisting arms

wrench the complacent bulk, the floor
slides underneath, and shells go past,
and the sand stirs its ribs, and more
leashes of bubbles break, and fast

the loins arched inward spurn to flight,
and on the opening of the eyes
invades the pale and paler light.
The swimmer and his body rise,

the dark descending and the dense
green dropping as the line goes by,
and drenched from two bright elements
the dripping shoulders take the sky.

The Islands

It is true, true
there are islands
available where there is nothing
to do but breathe in
bright air, plunge in the blue
water. No, really, they are there
within reach and means. A small
fishing boat (cabin cruiser) will carry
you across to your little hotel
bikini pool mini bar. What more
do you want? (Except maybe undo
that anchored self that says no
it's all in your head, all
this Elysian jazz. You have
to be dead first). And all
the time those little boats
go, to and fro, the happy
swingers or swindlers go
to take
the bright air and blue
water at those islands,
which are,
after all,
there.

Fall Guise

Promises keep slipping from the air, and scraps of
parchment lose their grip (nerves nerves), these has-beens,
these leftovers of summer tumble. Red waste

spreads at the feet of trees. Do not ask who. Times of
gorgeous mortality endure only in the times of
next year's calendars, but inscribe the wind with

unrecounted love affairs. Oh welcome
to the club, for every year we go through this
spectacular disintegration. This is what years are used for.

Waves

For Brewster Ghiselin

Ridges chipped, chiseled soften shape
as edges unsharpen, melt to farewell
stipple dimple and resolving keep
the large glassing contour, overswell

mounding to withdrawals, ripples riding
big bulges gather and reform, grow
foam flecks breaking kisses into air, sliding
down banks that heave ever higher, blow

threads on breaking crests, collapse, boil
between surges, wrinkle, heave open caves
of water, close slipping tons, recoil
and rise, breach and whiten, curl and crash, waves

waxing huge slammed and sombre, incessantly
disordering the thin topmost of the great quiet cold sea.

Cyclades

White houses spattered on hills,
terraced fields folded in valleys,
a skyline of windmills,
wind shut from crooked alleys;

feet in water, at peace
with all but weather and storm,
little Greek queens of the seas
keep themselves warm.

Protoprimavera

Spring with her messy poems makes
crocus shine in mud,
reluctant roots, reticent vines stir,
branches bud;

in cold upland corners iced
slabs strain into mist, seem
a seeming realized
in an impersonal dream.

Of Truth and Fact

Robins in dogwood toss
and tumble, flirt, alight
to mere touch of twigs, flutter, cross
their own invisible line of flight;

entity in air, valid
fact of immaterial motion, made
of speed and impulse, projected, rallied
back to base, lost, displayed

as agitation, torn air
without meaning, eternally
vanishing into nowhere:
but as true as tree.

Les Folies Françaises, ou les Dominos

de François Couperin

Voici
quelques folies,
dit-on, de France.
Je t'en fais don.
Il y a peut-être quelque signifiance?
Non.

La Virginité (sous le domino couleur d'invisible)

What color is no
color? I wear
no experience
nor mask of sense
but go
(this will pass)
bare
behind a costume of glass.

La Pudeur (sous le domino couleur de rose)

Cover the shape of the eyes
with pink
and shrink
from what I dare not realize.

L'Ardeur (sous le domino incarnat)

Reddish
is the color now
as of flesh,
or blood
in heart and head
that makes the warm
storm
of ardor glow.

L'Espérance (sous le domino vert)

It has not been given.
Wait

for wanted heaven.
Never too late
for what has never been.
I'll wait
in hope forever green.

La Fidélité (sous le domino bleu)

Even past
hope gone away
and lost,
I, in blue,
will stay
forever true.

La Persévérance (sous le domino gris de line)

Persistently
now in gray
I'll stay
and be
forever near
nor ever go away.

La Langueur (sous le domino violet)

Success
gluts. Failure dis-
heartens. Give
up all this
effort toward
life and live
none the less
bored.

La Coquètterie (sous différens dominos)

Such confections
as are these
turn their perfections

dressed to please
in all directions.

Les Vieux Galans et les Trésoriéres Surannées
(sous des dominos pourpres et feuilles mortes)

Old stuff,
purple and dead-leaf-
colored, fluff
and wire,
we know
the moves. Pity, that application
fails. By so
much (time, subtle thief!)
imagination
outstrips desire.

Les Coucous bénévoles (sous les dominos jaunes)

Shall we, in yellow
(not red or black) rave
if others crave
those sweets we own?
Our fellow-
sufferers are not few
nor all unknown.
Cuckoo!

La Jalousie taciturne (sous le domino gris de mauve)

No. Mine.
You dare
not touch
or stare
too much
at what's mine.
Such
mauve mood consorts
with life
cut by the self-held knife.
Which hurts.

La Frénésie, ou le Désespoir (sous le domino noir)

Black
is the color. See
the wrack
of old
(once green) hope, and feed
on sallow, cold
bile. Hope gone,
wear
across the bare
bone
black for despair.

L'Âme en Peine

Sometimes such troubles, stir-
ring my surface
as moods and confused colorings concur
to cloud the glass.

A Votive Offering

Amasis (King of Egypt) made a treaty of friendshp and alliance with the Cyrenaeans. And he decided to take a wife from there, whether because he wanted a Greek wife or because of his friendship for the Cyrenaeans in general. So he married one. Some say she was the daughter of Battus the son of Arcesilas, some say of Critobulus, a prominent citizen. Her name was Ladice. When Amasis went to bed with her, he was unable to have intercourse; he did with his other wives. When this happened again and again, Amasis said to this woman called Ladice: "Woman, you have bewitched me, and there is no way for you to escape the most wretched death any woman ever had." Ladice denied it but Amasis was not appeased, and she vowed in her mind to Aphrodite that, if Amasis had intercourse with her that night—for this would be the way out of her trouble—she would send a cult-image to Cyrene. And immediately after the vow Amasis had intercourse with her; and from then on every time he visited her he had intercourse, and he loved her very much after that. And Ladice duly fulfilled her vow; for she had a cult-image made and sent it to Cyrene, and there it was, intact down to my time, in front of the city of the Cyrenaeans.

Herodotus, *Histories* 2.181

Now that she had her prayer, now that the king
lay satisfied, now that she need not fear
the knife, rope, hatchet, pointed pole, bowstring,
or whatever method they might use to clear
unusable wives away with, and the sheath of red
terror she wore was dropped around her feet
like the real dress that she had worn to bed,
she tried to think why it had seemed so sweet
only to live, and lost the thought, and lay,
some kind of queen beside the sleeping man,
with nothing left to hope for in the day,
and all success since her short life began
the privilege to sleep, a favored wife,
by this gross, hearty king. And keep her life.

Spanish Succession

With acknowledgments to Southey

By Blenheim's battleground, old Casper's grandchildren questioned him
about that famous victory which had left the plowlands
sown with skulls. Why did they fight? Who made them so angry?

Old Casper, not one of the movers and shakers, had no real answer.
It was a question, who's going to sit on the throne of Spain,
that gathered the eagles, Eugene, Marlborough, old pros confronting

Villars and Boufflers, nearly their match, to ruffle the drummed armies,
to burst on the bewildered peasantry in Bavaria, the Low Countries
(who never knew what hit them, or why, because of that hypothetical

Spanish Successor) the reeking names of glory embattled
at Blenheim, Ramillies, Oudenarde, and Malplaquet, the grand heritage
of bloodstained banners worshipped in almost timeless regiments:

until the Allies against Louis all of a sudden realized
the man, it now turned out, they had been about to install on the Spanish
throne was quite unsuitable, and that was the treaty of Utrecht;

and in the villages of Flanders which had been the strategic
squares for those bloody chess combinations, the still-wondering yokels
were spared further gallantry and glory for almost a whole generation.

Disadvantages

The mocking-bird with a stick in his beak for the nest can not sing.
No centipede can move faster than his slowest leg.
You can not talk while swimming under water.
You can not row a boat while smoking a cigarette
nor embrace while driving a car.
Hope is a function of dissatisfaction;
ambition, of failure; anger, of love.
All these propositions are convertible into each other.

Form and Actuality

My times crush out. Prow's foam wings and the stern wash
carve water and disappear. The backstroke articulates
its vanishing pattern in the pool. Fragments of motion.

But gone stations are revisited and former hotel rooms
entered once more. Plane trees still dapple the streets by the river.
There is a design of redintegration, an ideal for perishing.

Lord, even Socrates Whitman and Herbert Hoover
were young once. Out of the billion biographies this one
moves at last to the term of its own formal arrangement.

But oh, those particulars.

Monadology

Secure inside our colored bolts we wheel
the drastic desert down. Waterless
swim huge waters. Frozen streams of steel
defend from turbulence, helplessness

in air's collapse. Flesh is armor
for soft and inward privacies against
violence of fiend and charmer.
Oh, ever closed and guarded, fenced

to face hate and hurt, how to assuage and blow
our hurricanes to calm, unpin
the self-sealed saving walls, forego
self, unlock the garden, and let strangers in?

Aspects of Time

The fourth dimension
for us, whatever us may be
will be was.

Ripens the grape. Shrivels it.
Or the claret in the cask, or the shape
of the boy or the girl, begins them matures them rots them.

Tears moon from earth,
loses stars in the hole.

Boils our beans
burns them.

Elicits the form of the stone into statue.
Made the stone.

Verb not noun or adjective,
constant and cruel.

Makes us what we will be are have been.
Creates us kills us.

Blood Relations

Red-river system inside us
comes and goes, returns and sets out
(awake asleep drunk)
not in our command,
orders itself,
us-not-us.

Makes blushes
colors. By denial
pallors.

Can be measured,
measures us,
our storms and calms,
our weather.

Falsified
as symbol of race guilt revenge.

Sharable. Beautiful. Indispensable.

Flesh Tones

What we got stuck with.
Housing for pains fevers phlegms cancers.
Endures incredibly
solid as statues, inwardly seething.

Devil's stronghold.
Matchless material for the torturer to work with.

Without breath (which is spirit)
or spirit (which is breath)
offal
or slab on the counter packaged in plastic
with by-products.

Resurrectable? To be recycled?
Scary. Scared.
But speeds curves colors tastes and textures,
look! Wonderful.

Bone Structure

Cleverly constructed concatenation of solids
whose fillings are pale fondant vital.

Subject of language's whimsy.
Funny.
Saw them cross them roll them.

Can ache break mend.

Bare they will frighten children and heroes.
Covered, the architect of beauty.
Without them, what shapeless hulks.

Dry in Ezekiel's valley, shall they live?

Eye Witness

Double strangers skull-lodged
half immersed in brine
white plastic-like globes
lashed lidded
centered with painted (water-color sort of)
pupae pupillae dolls korai.

                                   Most
sharp to pain, sharp to joy.

"Vile jelly."

Pop cross wall goggle crab
or soft melting, shine languish,
bat & beckon, flirt & flutter,
sheep's angel googoo
making.

Lord illuminator of the senses
like the Sun (Plato said)
brain's servant (not sole)
artist's driver's general's.

Without which
the still intelligent dark.

The Pearl

That swimmers of the rock conspired to weave
down the green shaken depth a flight
of turning loins and shoulders, and yet leave
forever captured in a shell of night

the globe of shining in the sand, shall mean
as idols mean in sleep, the truth
we carry sealed and quiet down the green
descent into a memory of youth.

This is the grammar of a dream, to mark
how the brown swimmers came and are,
pass and recoil from where the forgotten dark
turns pale again upon a buried star.

Western Ways

The simple-minded interstates have it now, and the motel-
and-filling-station towns: Holiday Inn, Best Western,
Quality, with Gulf and Texaco: the clean featureless

caravanserais: gas pools good beds sanitary
indifferent food. Oh yes, but beyond and outside lie
not only reservations and actual ranches but also

that special little town of the plains, at intervals strung on
the gleaming straightaway of the tracks. First seen miles off
green smudge, white silos at the southern edge, and the northern

marker of the water tower: Hays Russell Kit Carson:
oasis groves in the grasslands dropped there out of the nineties.
Yes, but sometimes the cruel flow-ways have passed them, leaving

a once proud road now secondary: coarse grass and broken
windows and festering boards, decay without circulation,
stare at us in squalid reproach, at us, the suburban

passers-through on our way from urban to coastal urban.
We might have lived another life by the silo and water tower.
Sometimes in the great desert the Greeks imagined Atlantis.

Tales from the Father of History

In Sparta, so they say,
was the ugliest baby girl, parents' despair.
A nurse took her every day
to the sanctuary of Helen. There

one day, a tall, stunning, gorgeously dressed
lady stood over the horrible little thing, smiled
at the protesting nurse, blessed
the baby and said: "This child

in a land of beautiful women shall grow
to be the loveliest of all." Of course, it was so.

In Egypt, the tiniest
of eggs hatched by the Nile
grows into the biggest beast:
the monstrous crocodile.

In Sparta, once again,
they had the best government: perfect, foursquare.
It had been the worst in the memory of men.

Read history with care.